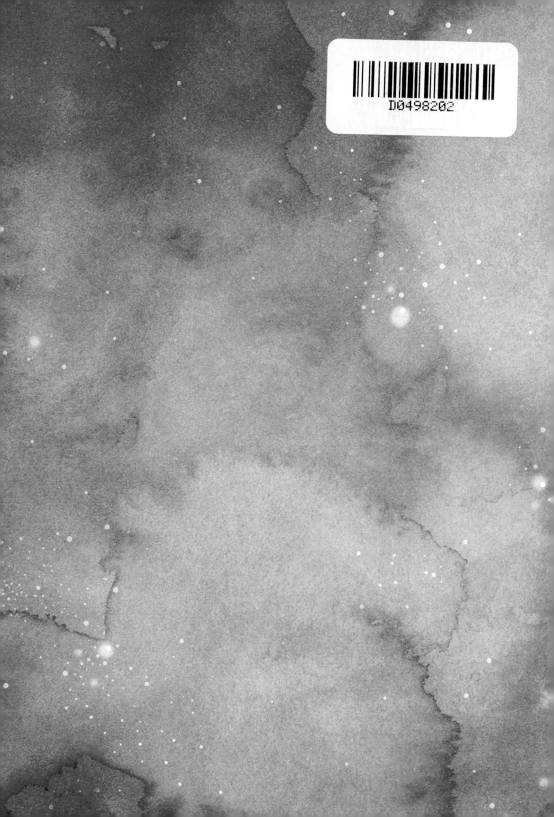

# Astrology for Black Girls

## A BEGINNER'S GUIDE FOR BLACK GIRLS WHO LOOK TO THE STARS

Written by
**Jordannah Elizabeth**

Illustrated by
**Chellie Carroll**

RP|KIDS
PHILADELPHIA

Running Press Kids
Hachette Book Group
1290 Avenue of the Americas, New York, NY 10104
www.runningpress.com/rpkids
@RP_Kids

Printed in China

First Edition: August 2022

Published by Running Press Kids, an imprint of Perseus Books, LLC,
a subsidiary of Hachette Book Group, Inc. The Running Press Kids name and logo
is a trademark of the Hachette Book Group.

The Hachette Speakers Bureau provides a wide range of authors for speaking events.
To find out more, go to www.hachettespeakersbureau.com or call (866) 376-6591.

The publisher is not responsible for websites (or their content)
that are not owned by the publisher.

Print book cover and interior design by Frances J. Soo Ping Chow.
Icons on page 98 copyright © Getty Images.

Library of Congress Cataloging-in-Publication Data
Names: Elizabeth, Jordannah, author. | Carroll, Chellie, illustrator.
Title: Astrology for Black girls : a beginner's guide for Black girls who look to the stars /
written by Jordannah Elizabeth ; illustrated by Chellie Carroll.
Description: First edition. | New York, NY : Running Press Kids, 2022. |
Includes bibliographical references. | Audience: Ages 8-12 | Summary: "A middle grade fully
illustrated book introducing the basics of astrology for black girl readers, including how
to look at natal charts, knowing sun, moon, and rising signs, and how to navigate studying
astrology while also keeping religion in one's life"—Provided by publisher.
Identifiers: LCCN 2021039304 (print) | LCCN 2021039305 (ebook) |
ISBN 9780762478576 (hardcover) | ISBN 9780762478583 (ebook) Subjects: LCSH:
Astrology—Juvenile literature. | African American girls—Juvenile literature.
Classification: LCC BF1714.A37 E45 2022 (print) | LCC BF1714.A37 (ebook) |
DDC 133.5—dc23 LC record available at https://lccn.loc.gov/2021039304
LC ebook record available at https://lccn.loc.gov/2021039305

ISBNs: 978-0-7624-7857-6 (hardcover), 978-0-7624-7858-3 (ebook)

APS

10  9  8  7  6  5  4  3  2  1

To the Black girls who don't fit the mold.
I'm always here for you.
And to my amazing mother.

—J. E.

# Contents

———————————•———————————

# Introduction

If you're reading this book, you probably have an interest in learning about other people, their thoughts, and what is going on inside their hearts. It's very possible that since you were a little child, you've been in touch with others' feelings and personalities, and how they relate to your own life. Do you ever wonder why you like to study all night before a test and can still get an A when your brother studies for weeks and can barely crack a C+? Do you wonder why your mom and grandmother seem to be so different from each other in the way they speak and get along with others, or why you and your best friend seem to be so alike that you know what each other is thinking?

Astrology is the study of the movement and interaction between the planets and the stars and how they affect people's lives and personalities. It can help you understand the dynamics between you and the people who are close to you.

As a Black girl, it's doubly important that you learn the skills of astrology to help you become more aware of the world around you. That's because you're unique and special, with your hairstyle, favorite music, and dance moves. And those things that make you so special might also make people around you struggle to know where you're coming from. This book can help you be your very best self and find the ways you differ and stand out in the world. It can also help you discover how similar you are to people who may not look like you or come from your same background.

I have been interested in astrology since I was about twelve years old. My mother would take me to bookstores, and I would sit in the aisles for hours reading about my astrological sign—Libra—so I could get to know myself better and more deeply. As I read more and more about astrology, I learned almost everything there is to know about signs and about the traits that make people who they are.

Now, twenty years later, I can figure out someone's sign just by listening to them speak. I can look at someone's facial features, the way they laugh, the questions they ask, and the way they communicate, and I can know if they are a Leo, Pisces, or any of the other signs. I've learned to use astrology as a tool to help me get to know people better. By knowing people's signs, I have instant general knowledge about their personalities and their likes and dislikes. With this knowledge, I can communicate with others and find ways to avoid hurting people's feelings by mistake! If I know someone is a Cancer, I know they have soft and deep emotions, so I try to speak kind words. If I needed to address an issue, I'd try to say things in a way that the person doesn't feel like they've done something wrong. Cancers have a hard time with criticism. It hurts their feelings when they think they've done something that might hurt another person.

When I was first learning about astrology, though, the one thing I didn't have was a book that was made for Black girls like me. And now, as an adult, I want to share all the amazing things I've learned over many years with young girls who want to live life with valuable information about people and how they connect with the planets and stars in the sky.

As you study astrology more, you should be able to understand more deeply what makes people the way they are. Astrology may not be for everyone, but I know in my heart that it is definitely for you and all the Black girls in the world who seek to learn about this cosmic journey we are on.

You are on a path of discovery! When anyone begins a new path, things can seem hard to learn and understand. But as you read this book over and over, you'll begin to remember what you've read, and you will be able to talk to your friends and family about this wonderful information. You can even help them on their journeys if they choose to follow this path too.

*Astrology for Black Girls* isn't about telling you exactly who you are; rather, it's about showing you a new way of seeing the world. Don't be shy or ashamed of being different. Not everyone is going to understand your interest in astrology because it's not for everyone. This is for *you*, and this book will give you the tools to follow your heart and to go after anything and everything you truly dream about.

The most important thing to know about this book is that, in the end, it exists for you to have fun! Astrology *is* fun, and if you love to read, you'll spend hours with your nose buried in this book, uncovering secrets about yourself. You deserve to create a relationship with who you are deep inside and to better understand how you move about the world. Give this life all you've got, and you will be rewarded with wisdom and self-awareness. Enjoy each day, and never let anyone tell you that you can't learn all there is to know about the sky above you or the Earth your beautiful feet are planted on!

Part One

# CHOOSING TO EXPLORE ASTROLOGY

# CHAPTER ONE

# Black Girl Astrology

## It's Okay, Astrology Isn't Just for White People

"Astrology is for white people!"

Don't be surprised if you hear this as you begin to learn about astrology. It's true that for many years, this study has been led by white astrologers, but we are living in a different time now. Black astrologers like Sam Reynolds, the world's leading Black astrologer and founder of Unlock Astrology; Adama Sesay, who is also a "cosmic alchemist" and founder of Lilith Astrology; Mecca Woods, an astrology teacher who gives readings through her site, My Life Created; Kirah Tabourn, a writer and astrology instructor, and founder of the Strology; and others are leading the way in the new world of astrology.

Black people exploring Western astrology can be traced back hundreds of years. Black astronomer and mathematician Benjamin Banneker, born in 1731, created a yearly almanac in 1792 to track the movements of the stars and the best times for farming. Along with astronomy and mathematical analysis, Banneker also included a bit of astrological information so farmers would know how the stars would affect them personally. Today, astrologers still study and use this almanac to learn more about astrological techniques. So it's important to remember: Black people have been a part of the history of astrology for centuries!

As you start to learn more about astrology, try not to worry about what other people say. Just because people don't know about astrology's history and all the amazing Black astrologers who exist today doesn't mean that they can tell you that only white people study and practice astrology. They clearly just don't know all the facts.

Be proud of being an inquisitive, smart, strong, and curious Black girl who is interested in and excited to learn more about the stars and how people relate to them.

If someone tells you that you can't be into astrology because you are Black, you can let them know that there are many Black people all over the world who believe that the stars and planets can show you all about the energy of each day. Astrology can also help you figure out which friends you'll get along with the best and why you have a loving personality or a strong temper.

Don't be afraid to stand up for yourself. You have the power to tell and show other people that you can do anything no matter your race. If they laugh at you or continue to argue with you about your interests, don't let it get you down. You don't have to tell everyone that you are interested in astrology. Stick to the people who are respectful and supportive of what you like. You have nothing to prove; you are amazing just the way you are.

And always remember: Astrology is *not* just for white people!

CHAPTER TWO

# Astrology & Religion

## You Can Have Faith *and* Be an Astrologer!

A strology is not a religion. Religion is a belief system based on the worship of a god, gods, or goddesses that directly affects the lives of human beings. Though astrology is tied to the traits and powers of Greek and Roman gods and goddesses, you are not required to worship them. They are seen as symbols. Astrology is the study of the movement and placement of celestial bodies (planets, stars, and asteroids) in the sky and how that relates to and affects human lives. It's like how meteorologists can predict the weather based on the movement and position of air, heat, rain, and clouds.

Some religions, such as Christianity, might frown upon astrology because divination (the prediction of events that are going to happen through external tools) does not fit the mold of the teachings of that particular religion. But there is a story in the Bible about the Three Wise Men who followed the Star of Bethlehem, a bright eastern star, to find and bless baby Jesus soon after he was born. This is the reason why many people put a star on top of their Christmas trees. So even in Christianity, there are stories of how the stars played an important role in religion.

Many Eastern religions, like Hinduism, strongly believe in astrology and use it to predict the perfect time for special events like weddings. They also use astrology to find out if a couple is compatible (meaning if they will get along with each other) before they are married to ensure a long and happy life together.

Every religion has a different relationship with astrology, but always remember that you can have faith in God, follow your religion, *and* still love learning about the planets and stars.

Just because you study astrology doesn't mean you have to skip out of Sunday church service or worshipping at your local mosque. You can do both! If your family members are very traditional and worry about you studying astrology, you can promise them that you still respect what they believe in, and you want to be a part of all they have to teach you. You can tell them that you are interested in astrology because it's a new way of seeing the world. It is always truly up to you what you believe in, but just make sure you understand that you don't have to give up your faith in a higher power to pursue astrology.

Believing in gods (and goddesses) can bring you joy and comfort in knowing that there is a higher, invisible power that watches over you and protects you from harm. Gods have always been a way for human beings to find answers to the meaning of life and to teach them how to overcome difficult times through prayer and devotion. We can ask the gods to bring us good outcomes in situations that are troubling to us. We can ask for healing from illnesses and worship them through music and rituals to show how grateful we are for their presence in our lives.

In ancient astrology, Roman gods were deeply intertwined in its ideology. For instance, Mars is the God of War and rules Aries. Because of this, Aries takes on a bit of the personality and powers of Mars. Aries people love to challenge others and are great competitors. They have quick tempers and fiery, strong styles of communication. Being ruled by Mars doesn't really mean Aries people love war, but they certainly don't shy away from tough obstacles and arguments.

Again, astrology is not a religion! You don't have to worship Mars or even believe he is real. Mars is more of a symbol used to help us understand how the planet and the traits of the Roman god can affect events in people's lives.

As you get older, you will understand more about your own faith and religion and will be able to choose what you do and do not believe in. It is always good to learn about different ways of seeing the world. For now, it is very important to trust your family and respect the beliefs and religion of your parents even if you do not agree. They work hard to take care of you and do their best to show you how to live a safe and happy life. It is a bonus if your parents love astrology, of course. They can keep you company while you study and can help you become a great astrologer.

If you do not live with your parents or don't know who they are, that's okay! Astrology can help you find out more about yourself, which is a great way to learn how to have self-love.

If you do not believe in a god or don't have a religious family, that's perfectly fine too! You are not required to have a religious faith to study the workings of the planets and stars.

# CHAPTER THREE

# Family & Astrology

## Learning More from Your Parents and Family

The information in this book has been carefully compiled and organized to help you learn and understand the basics of astrology. Most people know their Sun signs because they are based in modern astrology. All the horoscopes you see in magazines and online focus on the Sun signs, so make sure you know when people tell you their sign that they are usually telling you their Sun sign only. Once you understand the Sun sign traits, move on to the Moon signs, then the Rising signs, then study the elements, quadruplicities, and the planets and houses!

In order to find out your Rising sign, you will need to know exactly when and where you were born. If you live with your mom, dad, or other family members, they will need to help you find your birth certificate so they can tell you the exact time you were born. If you moved away from the city or country you were born in, you'll need to know the spelling of the country and city of your birth so you can calculate your Rising sign. Your Rising sign is the sign that was rising on the eastern horizon the moment you were born.

Each Rising sign moves into a different sign in your astrology chart every two hours (you will learn more about charts in later chapters!). For example, if you were born at 2:37 p.m. but simply guessed that you were born at noon, you may not be able to calculate your correct Rising sign. This is why it is important that your parents or guardians help you find your birth certificate because it has all the information you need to know. If your family members can't find it, they can access your birth certificate online and purchase a copy for you. It does cost money, so if they can't afford it, that's okay! While you won't be able to know your exact Rising sign, you can figure out your Sun and Moon signs without knowing your birth time. Don't feel discouraged! You can still learn a good deal about yourself without knowing your Rising sign.

You can also ask your family members for their birthdays so you can read about their signs. Knowing other people's birthdays will help you study and understand your personality traits and how you will relate to others' personalities according to their signs. If your mom loves dancing, throwing parties, and being the center of attention, she may be a Leo. If your dad is a stay-at-home dad and loves to be around family, he may be a Taurus.

Astrology isn't all about personalities though. As you get more advanced in reading the stars and the planets, you'll learn that the stars can tell you about the mood and energy of certain days. This book focuses on the Sun, Moon, and Rising signs, planets, and houses, which will prepare you to read astrology birth charts. Birth charts are like maps of people's lives. They show where the planets and stars were when you were born, and you can also find out how the celestial bodies are affecting you every day. Be open to every new thing that you learn!

Your family can be a wonderful help as you begin your exploration about the stars and planets. If you don't have a good relationship with your family or don't have many friends, you can find your favorite musician's or movie star's birthday by searching their name online. And then you can practice reading about their signs and personalities. There are so many cool celebrities, writers, artists, and musicians to choose from, you'll never get tired of learning about their signs!

The main thing to remember as you begin to learn astrology is to have fun!

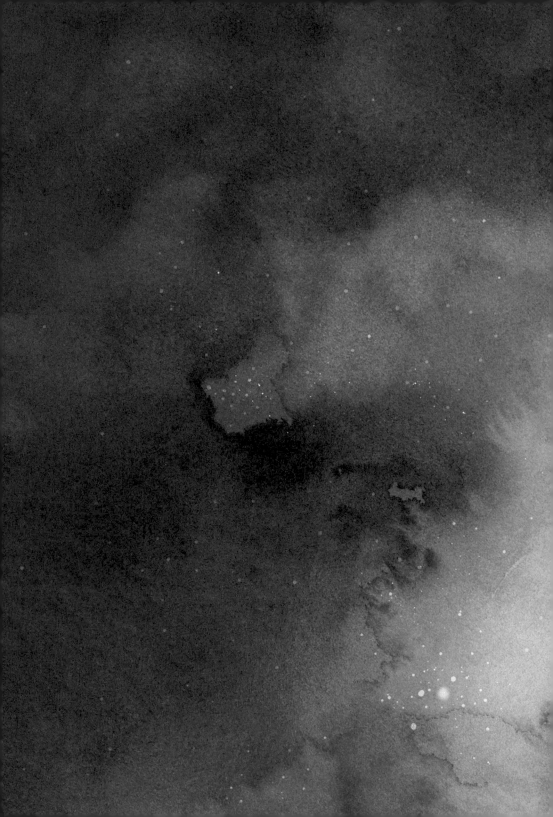

Part Two

# WHERE
# TO BEGIN?

## UNDERSTANDING THE FUN FOUNDATIONS
## OF ASTROLOGICAL STUDY

ARIES

TAURUS

GEMINI

CANCER

LEO

VIRGO

LIBRA

SCORPIO

SAGITTARIUS

CAPRICORN

AQUARIUS

PISCES

# CHAPTER FOUR

# The Zodiac Signs & Your Astrology Chart

Zodiac signs are clusters of stars in the sky that are called constellations. Each cluster has its own special shape and formation that sit across the ecliptic. The ecliptic is an imaginary line formed by the circular path of the Sun as it moves across the sky. The Sun doesn't actually move, but as the Earth orbits the Sun once per year, the Sun seems to move across the sky through the twelve constellations of the Zodiac. It takes the Sun one year to pass through the entire ecliptic. Ancient cultures noticed that certain things would happen to people on Earth as the Sun moved through this collection of stars—or "signs"—and they eventually created astrology to explain the different moods and influences that many people were experiencing at the same time. People born under the same Zodiac constellation seemed to have similar personalities and ways of thinking.

The planets of the solar system (and the orbit of planets around the Sun) are mostly near the ecliptic, so the planets also have different effects on the people of Earth. This is why the movement of the Sun, Moon, and the planets through different Zodiac signs are very important to astrological study. There are countless other constellations and stars in the universe, and some are recognized by astrologers of today. But astrologers mostly focus on the Sun, Moon, and Rising signs (which you will learn about in part three) and how they relate to the Zodiac.

Astrologers use charts that show where the Sun, the Moon, and the planets are placed at the time of your birth. The charts also reveal influences based on the angles of the planets in relationship to one another. These angles are called aspects. They are quite complicated, so they won't be covered in depth in this guide. This book mainly focuses on the Big Three or the Magic Three: Sun, Moon, and Rising signs and their connection with the twelve Zodiac signs.

Your astrology birth chart, which is also called a natal chart, is a view of where all the planets were in the paths around the Sun at the exact time of your birth. This birth chart shows the precise positions of where the planets and constellations were in the sky the very moment you were born. Knowing the positions of the Sun, Moon, and planets during the time of your birth gives you important information about your personality, your emotional reactions to circumstances, and what your career and the nature of your relationships with your friends and family may be like.

Your birth chart is constructed with four different components: signs, houses, planets, and aspects, or angles. As a beginner, you do not have to know everything all at once. You can memorize the traits of the planets, signs, and houses before you go deeply into aspects. Knowing what they represent by heart will make it easier to understand how the angles and connections between planets work and what they can mean.

**ARIES**
Fire • Cardinal • Masculine

**TAURUS**
Earth • Fixed • Feminine

**GEMINI**
Air • Mutable • Masculine

**CANCER**
Water • Cardinal • Feminine

**LEO**
Fire • Fixed • Masculine

**VIRGO**
Earth • Mutable • Feminine

**LIBRA**
Air • Cardinal • Masculine

**SCORPIO**
Water • Fixed • Feminine

**SAGITTARIUS**
Fire • Mutable • Masculine

**CAPRICORN**
Earth • Cardinal • Feminine

**AQUARIUS**
Air • Fixed • Masculine

**PISCES**
Water • Mutable • Feminine

CHAPTER FIVE

# The Elements (Triplicities) & Quadruplicities

T he Zodiac is made up of twelve signs that are broken into four elemental categories. The elements are also called triplicities. Each element—earth, air, fire, and water—is a representation of the sign's temperament, which defines how calm, or not so calm, you are in your daily life. Earth and Water signs express themselves inwardly and are more introverted while Fire and Air signs have more outward and outgoing personalities. Each element is assigned to three astrology signs: Aries, Leo, and Sagittarius are Fire signs; Cancer, Scorpio, and Pisces are Water signs; Gemini, Libra, and Aquarius are Air signs; and Taurus, Virgo, and Capricorn are Earth signs. Each element can help you define how a particular person will approach life.

**Earth Signs** (Taurus, Virgo, and Capricorn) have the most grounded personalities of the elements. If you are an Earth sign, your down-to-earth approach to life makes you practical and able to tackle life by the guidance of your senses. You trust what you can feel, taste, see, touch, and hear, and you use your logic and what you know of the material world to make decisions. Earth signs want a stable home and environment and don't like surprises!

**Air Signs** (Gemini, Libra, and Aquarius) are the best communicators of all the elements. As an Air sign, you like to think about things before you express your opinions. You may be very good at writing, and you love to be around people who are interesting and can hold good conversations. You like to use your head more than your heart, and that can make it difficult to express your emotions at times. You're more about what's going on in your mind, and this makes you a very intelligent person who loves to learn and share information!

**Water Signs** (Cancer, Scorpio, and Pisces) are very sensitive and are motivated to act by what they feel. If you are a Water sign, you have a strong intuition, which means you can tap into what others are thinking and understand their needs without them telling you what they are. This also means you are easily affected by other people's moods. If someone close to you is sad, you may feel sad; if they are excited or happy, you will feel this energy and may feel happy as well. Feelings are key components in the life of a Water sign person!

**Fire Signs** (Aries, Leo, and Sagittarius) are intensely passionate people who love adventure. If you are a Fire sign you are more interested in showing outward emotions and exploring the world with lively zeal. You have an outgoing personality and are assertive, which means you will act on things that are getting in the way of what you want. You gain power from your warm, fiery, spontaneous inner strength!

# QUADRUPLICITIES

The qualities or quadruplicities of the Zodiac are broken up into three categories of four signs each: cardinal, fixed, and mutable. They represent your attitude and how you communicate and interact with the world around. Cardinal signs (Aries, Cancer, Libra, Capricorn) fall at the beginning of every season, such as the spring, summer, fall, and winter. People born under these signs are leaders and self-starters. The fixed signs (Taurus, Leo, Scorpio, Aquarius) are placed in the center of every season, so people born under these signs are stable and centered. This means they are grounded and like to think and plan before they act. Mutable signs (Gemini, Virgo, Sagittarius, Pisces) fall at the end of each season. Mutable sign people are good at preparing those around them for things to end. They create a safe environment for change to come and for the things of the past to end.

## CARDINAL

| ARIES | CANCER | CAPRICORN | LIBRA |

Cardinal Signs (Aries, Cancer, Libra, and Capricorn) are geared toward initiation, meaning these people are active, born leaders who like to be the spark that gets things going. The cardinal signs also represent the beginning of the four seasons. Aries represents spring (vernal equinox), Cancer is summer (summer solstice), Libra is fall (autumnal equinox), and Capricorn is winter (winter solstice).

## FIXED

| TAURUS | LEO | SCORPIO | AQUARIUS |

**Fixed Signs** (Taurus, Leo, Scorpio, and Aquarius) are strong-willed people who are motivated by what they value. Fixed signs do not like change. They like to save and preserve things. For example, don't expect a fixed sign person to share their favorite video game or snack with you.

## MUTABLE

| SAGITTARIUS | VIRGO | GEMINI | PISCES |

**Mutable Signs** (Gemini, Virgo, Sagittarius, and Pisces) are flexible people, meaning they are easy to get along with and are good listeners. They like to share ideas and can go with the flow in all sorts of different environments.

# CHAPTER SIX

# The Houses

Your astrology birth chart looks like a circle divided into twelve sections, which are called houses. The houses represent who you are as "self" and move outward, explaining your place in your family in your home, and in society. During the exact time you were born, the planets all fell into specific houses and signs. The position of the houses, signs, and planets combined to tell the story of who you are and the challenges, triumphs, and gifts you will encounter throughout your life.

To find your first house you will look for the small symbol "AC" (meaning Ascendant) in the chart, which corresponds to your Rising sign. Then, you will move counterclockwise through each section, which will be your second, third, fourth houses and so on. You can also find numbers on the inside circle of the wheel. They will show you the numbers of the houses as well.

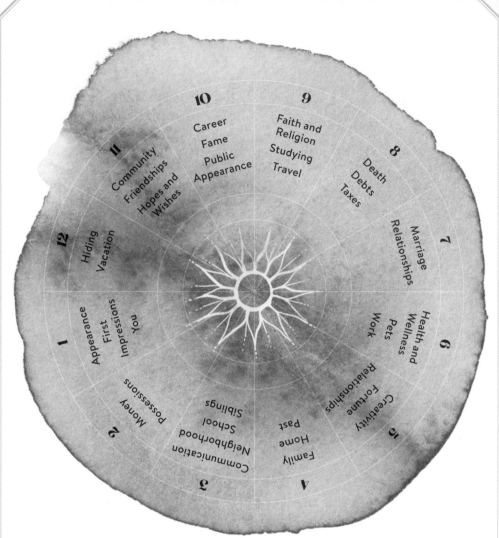

*Here's a look at how the
houses are placed in the birth chart.*

Your Rising sign or Ascendant sign is always going to rule your first house.
If your Rising sign is Capricorn, that will rule your first house. Aquarius will
rule your second house because Aquarius comes after Capricorn; that means
Pisces will rule your third house. This will go on through all twelve houses.

Because the second house rules money and resources and Aquarius represents a unique and innovative thinker, you will have many different and out-of-the-box ways of making money and attracting material possessions.

In ancient astrology, the sign ruler of the houses is determined by which planet ruling a Zodiac sign sits on the cusp of each house. A cusp is a position that sits between each house and is the ending of one house and the beginning of the next. For now, get to know what the houses mean, and you will soon find out how the planets and signs work with them.

# FIRST HOUSE

The first house of your birth chart is also called the Ascendant, and it represents the first impression you make on others. It marks the sign that was rising on the eastern horizon when you were born. Your Rising sign reflects who you are to the outer world and how you behave when you meet new people or find yourself in a new environment. For example, if your Sun sign is Libra and your Rising sign is Virgo, you will show Virgo-like personality traits to people when you first meet them. The first house shows the way you approach other people and your plans, the general mood in your life, your outward appearance, your personality type, your independence, and your temperament.

## SECOND HOUSE

The second house represents your resources, which means all the material things you have and how you get them. As you get older, it will help show how you'll make money and how you'll go about getting the things that you need to make you feel safe and secure. It also represents the skills you have that will help you succeed and get the things you need in your life. The second house can reveal the way you deal with money, finances, and wealth; it also shows your talent and abilities.

## THIRD HOUSE

The third house reveals your communication skills—how you learn, write, and speak. It also helps you find out how you get along with your siblings (if you have any), how you interact with your neighbors, or how you deal with short trips to places that are close to your home. The third house can teach you about the short trips you will take, your everyday experiences, the way you learn, the power of your expression, and the way you think.

## FOURTH HOUSE

The fourth house is the house of home and family and can show how you get along with your mother and father or other caregivers. It is good to find out about this house when you are young because it teaches you about your early life experiences with your family. It is also the house of ancestry, meaning it shows information about your connection with members of your family who are older, like your grandmother and those who came before her. The fourth house represents tradition, the home, your dreams, your need for security, and the way in which you live.

## FIFTH HOUSE

The fifth house reveals your creativity, how you express yourself, and how you love others. It shows how you play, how you love the people around you, and what entertains you. It also represents your relationships with siblings, family, and friends. You can find out what makes you happy and the wonderful things that you enjoy. It is also the house that is associated with theater, music, and all things artistic! The fifth house represents the way in which you show who you are, your self-expression, your joy in life, your playfulness and pleasure.

## SIXTH HOUSE

The sixth house represents your health and the environment in which you work. You can find out the way you like to take care of your health and well-being and the ways you best work with others. The sixth house is also known as the house of service, which tells you how you go about helping others in your life. The sixth house can reveal your basic physical health, your place of work, and the relationship between your body and mind, and the way in which you work.

## SEVENTH HOUSE

The seventh house is the house of relationships, partnerships, and marriage. You can find out how you function and interact with your closest one-on-one relationships like your friends and schoolmates. You can also see the kinds of relationships you will have with close coworkers when you get old enough to work a job. And while you are too young for marriage, you can peer into the future and see how you will behave in relationships with people you may fall in love with. The seventh house is the house of marriage, long-lasting relationships, the way in which you give and receive love, and the way you behave within a relationship.

## EIGHTH HOUSE

The eighth house can be scary for some because it is the house of death. But don't let that frighten you! It is the house that shows where and how you keep your deepest secrets. It is also the house of finances and taxes, which is something you won't have to worry about for many years. But it is good to know how you will handle money and relationships intuitively. The eighth house represents death and rebirth, transformation, overcoming difficulties in life, and other people's material possessions and money.

## NINTH HOUSE

The ninth house represents religion, philosophy, legal affairs, and long-distance travel. It can show how you feel if or when you go to religious sermons at a church, mosque, temple, or synagogue. Your philosophy of life will reveal how you think about the world around you. It can also show whether you will travel to faraway places and how those places will affect your outlook on life. The ninth house can tell you more about your search for truth and meaning in life. It can also tell you more about religion, higher education, God, and your philosophy of life.

## TENTH HOUSE

The tenth house can teach you about your future career, your reputation, and your interactions as a public citizen. This house can also show you your relationships with your community members. It shows your public standing in the larger realm of your culture and if you will be loved, disliked, or how you will be treated by people around you. You can find out if you will be famous and successful on a world stage, and what your career will be once you are an adult. The tenth house can show you your relationship to fame, your calling, your social life, public recognition, your career, success in life, and responsibility.

## ELEVENTH HOUSE

The eleventh house reveals how you interact with others through your friendships, groups, and social organizations, as well as how those interactions affect you. Maybe you will grow up to be a part of an environmental cause, or maybe you'll lean toward becoming friends with those who believe in the same things you do. It is important to know how you will find your place in group settings and which ways your friends and allies will accept you. The eleventh house reveals how you interact with groups, friendships, and teams; it also reveals how you help others.

## TWELFTH HOUSE

The twelfth house represents spirituality and the psychic world. It has a lot to do with the deep inner knowledge you have and your connection with the invisible spiritual world that exists around you. It is also the house of hidden enemies and is called the house of un-doing. This is the house that will reveal the things that you can't see with your eyes but must instead sense with your inner self. The twelfth house can show your inner life's connection with mysticism, and the way in which you withdraw from the world. This house also represents secrets, enemies, purification, and isolation.

# CHAPTER SEVEN

# The Four Quadrants & the Angles

The houses are broken up into four parts, called quadrants, on a birth chart. Each quadrant has an individual meaning connected to the placements of the houses.

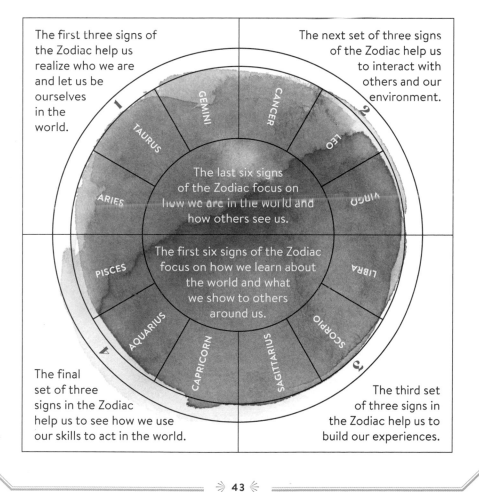

The first three signs of the Zodiac help us realize who we are and let us be ourselves in the world.

The next set of three signs of the Zodiac help us to interact with others and our environment.

The last six signs of the Zodiac focus on how we are in the world and how others see us.

The first six signs of the Zodiac focus on how we learn about the world and what we show to others around us.

The final set of three signs in the Zodiac help us to see how we use our skills to act in the world.

The third set of three signs in the Zodiac help us to build our experiences.

GEMINI · CANCER · TAURUS · LEO · ARIES · VIRGO · PISCES · LIBRA · AQUARIUS · CAPRICORN · SAGITTARIUS · SCORPIO

**Quadrant 1, Houses 1–3, Awareness of Self.** This quadrant represents the self, self-image, and self-worth. It combines your personality, communication style, and value systems, which is what you believe in, what you can do on this Earth, and how it relates to who you are to the outside world.

**Quadrant 2, Houses 4–6, Connecting with Your Environment.** The second quadrant shows how you relate to your friends, family, and larger groups. It shows who you are in relation to those close to you. This quadrant also deals with creativity and shows how you deal with conflicts and disagreements in your life.

**Quadrant 3, Houses 7–9, Awareness of Others.** The third quadrant reveals your connection with philosophy and religion, and how these parts of your life help or hurt your relationships. This quadrant shows how you cooperate with others (their philosophies and ways they see the world), and how you balance your need for individuality.

**Quadrant 4, Houses 10–12, Connecting with Society.** The fourth quadrant relates to you and your society (meaning "everyone is together"). While the other quadrants focus on you, houses 10–12 relate to you mixed in with everyone and everything, including how you participate in the world outside you.

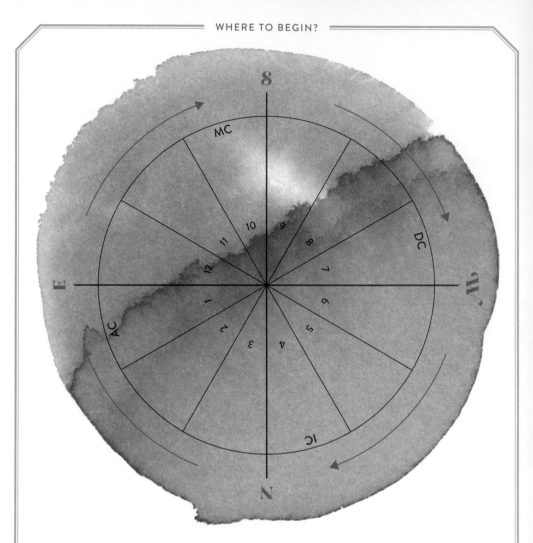

## THE ANGLES

The Ascendant, Descendant, Midheaven, and Imum Coeli are the four angles of the astrology chart. The planets that land on these points of the chart help define a person's personality. The planets that are connected to these points are called "angular planets."

The astrology chart is divided into upper and lower halves that represent the Ascendant and Descendant portions of the chart. The upper half of the chart symbolizes your inner spirit or consciousness, and the lower half is connected to what you experience in the outer world or what's going on outside your mind and body. The Midheaven and Imum Coeli line divides the astrology chart into Eastern and Western hemispheres. The Eastern hemisphere is connected to the active self, and the Western hemisphere shows the influences people have on your life.

The Zodiac sign that falls on the Ascendent (AC) angle in your chart is called your Rising sign. It reveals the way you act in new situations and the way you approach life through your personality. The planet that lands on your Ascendant will also affect your personality. The Ascendant is always in the first house of your chart. You will learn more about planets in the next chapter.

The Imum Coeli (IC) portion of the chart relates to your heritage, your home, and your family. When a planet is near your IC it will affect where you live, who you live with, and how you get along in your environment. It can also affect your feelings about where you were born and how your home has had a positive or negative influence in your life.

The Descendant (DC) focuses on other people. The planets that are near your Descendant will color the way you experience other people, and the traits of those planets will help you understand how others in your life have an impact on your relationship to your external world.

The Midheaven (MC) represents your social standing, the career you will have when you grow up, and how others see you (in other words, your reputation). You will learn about the characteristics of your public life, and any planet that is near your Midheaven will give you a clearer view of how others' opinions of you will define you as a person.

# CHAPTER EIGHT

# The Planets

W hen you have a good understanding of the planetary cycles and the attributes of each planet, you can see how they are going to affect your life. You won't be able to know exactly what will happen to you, but you will be able to read how the energies of the planets will bring about certain events. Every planet in the solar system has its own timing and pace when orbiting the Sun. Once you study and learn the cycles of the planets in the solar system, you will begin to see how each planet's movement affects your life. When you observe these planets over years, you will begin to memorize each planet's impact and know when to plan special events and make big decisions depending on the planet's placements and orbits.

Each planet's cycle is very different! For example, Mercury's cycle revolves around the Sun and goes around the entire Zodiac in 88 days. In contrast, Pluto takes 250 years to make it around the entire Zodiac chart. So, Pluto will stay in each sign for 21 to 31 years. We will look more deeply into Pluto's orbit and its effects on each sign later in this book. But for now, we will focus on the inner, or personal, planets: Mercury, Venus, and Mars along with the Moon. These planets orbit the Sun much faster than the outer planets and have more of an immediate effect on everyday life. The outer planets are Jupiter, Saturn, Uranus, Neptune, and Pluto.

When it comes to your chart, you will find out which planets fall in each house by reading your chart. If Mercury, the planet of communication, falls in your third house (which also represents how you communicate), you will most likely be a natural writer, or maybe a speaker with a wonderful way with words and clear expression! If Venus, which is the planet of love and relationships, is in your eleventh house (which represents groups, community, and social organizations), you will very likely love being around groups of people, and they will love you in return!

The planets are also associated with archetypes; for example, Mercury is the Messenger, and Mars is the Warrior. Think of the archetypes as actors and actresses in a play. They will act out these behaviors in the theater of life. The planets also rule certain astrological signs, days of the week, houses, and parts of the body. Whatever the planet represents, its effects will shine through in these placements and parts of each human being.

The planets are also associated with colors. For example, Mercury rules communication. If you want to have better communication, you can plan to send an email on a Wednesday while wearing the color yellow to help remind you that you are going to send a clear and well written message with certainty!

Without the planets, astrology would not exist. Their movements across the sky and through the solar system help you see what will be going on in the world and in many facets of life!

# INNER PLANETS

## MERCURY
### THE ONE WHO SENDS MESSAGES

Planet Cycle: Revolves around the Sun every 88 days
Sign Ruler: Gemini and Virgo
Day of the Week: Wednesday
House Ruler: Third and Sixth
Color: Yellow
The Body: Lungs, arms, hands

Mercury is known as the planet of communication. Mercury reveals the way we learn, write, speak, and think! It is the planet that helps you gather and organize information you take in, and it also organizes the realm of your subconscious. Mercury may support you in being talented with words—whether it is through speaking or writing. You have a sharp intellect and know how to express the thoughts you have in your mind.

# VENUS

## THE TRUEST ARTIST

**Planet Cycle:** Revolves around the Sun every 224½ days
**Sign Ruler:** Taurus and Libra
**Day of the Week:** Friday
**House Ruler:** Second and Seventh
**Color:** Green
**The Body:** Voice, skin, kidneys

Venus is the planet of love and of the arts. Being born under Venus will explain how you behave in love relationships, how you get along with others, and how you showcase your natural artistic side. Venus also represents your feminine side and how you express your feminine nature. Venus can help you find out what pleases you in life. If you have a positive Venus aspect in your chart, you are likely to get along with others nicely and to attract people with the loving and pleasant elements of your personality.

# MARS

## THE POWERFUL WARRIOR

Planet Cycle: **Revolves around the Sun every 22 months**
Sign Ruler: **Aries**
Day of the Week: **Tuesday**
House Ruler: **First**
Color: **Ruby**
The Body: **Blood, muscles**

While Venus relates to your natural feminine side, Mars represents the masculine warrior spirit that lives inside you. Mars is where you will find your courage and strength. This planet helps explain how you go about getting what you want and how you assert yourself in the world. If you have a positive Mars in your chart, you can be strong-willed, ambitious, and move through life with self-assurance. You can get what you want by confidently going after it!

# OUTER PLANETS

## JUPITER
### THE NEED FOR EXPANSION

Planet Cycle: Spends 1 year in each sign, a 12-year cycle
Sign Ruler: Sagittarius
Day of the Week: Thursday
House Ruler: Ninth
Color: Dark blue
The Body: Thighs, liver

Jupiter represents luck, generosity, and prosperity. This planet helps you understand the way you explore and grow by learning from positive experiences. It is the planet of expansion. This means if you have a positive Jupiter in your chart, you may be very interested in having good exchanges with people by being generous and helpful. Jupiter can show your purpose in life and help you identify the positive aspects that help you improve yourself and become a better person.

# SATURN

## THE RESPONSIBLE ONE, THE MASTER OF TASKS

Planet Cycle: Spends 2½ years in each sign, a 29½-year cycle
Sign Ruler: Capricorn
Day of the Week: Saturday
House Ruler: Tenth
Color: Black, gray
The Body: Knees, bones, teeth

Saturn rules the areas of life that are focused on responsibility, commitment, discipline, and things that we feel we "should do" compared to the things that we want to do. Some believe that Saturn is a harsh planet and one that is all about rules. But the good thing about having Saturn in your chart is that it helps you deal with challenges and difficult aspects of your environment and personality. It gives you the strength to handle limitations and boundaries that can seem like they are holding you back, but that are actually keeping you from going overboard or doing too much. This, in turn, can be seen as protection from situations that call for you to do things safely and responsibly.

# URANUS

## THE ONE WHO BRINGS AWAKENINGS

**Planet Cycle:** Spends 7 years in each sign, an 84-year cycle
**Sign Ruler:** Aquarius (modern ruler)
**House Ruler:** Eleventh
**Color:** Aquamarine
**The Body:** Nervous system, thyroid

Uranus, which is the very first outer planet of the Zodiac, is a revolutionary planet that represents individuality and the freedom to change and evolve into the best version of yourself! This planet is the planet of "awakenings" and can cause you to break away from things that seem normal and stale. You will find yourself being rebellious and dreaming of doing things differently from others when this planet is strong in your chart. This planet also rules technology and astrology, which means you may find yourself wanting to learn about these things more deeply. Uranus promotes resourcefulness that helps you find the tools to achieve your original goals as well as an individual-istic way of living your life!

# NEPTUNE
## A VISIONARY AND MISTAKE

**Planet Cycle:** Spends 14 years in each sign, a 168-year cycle
**Sign Ruler:** Pisces
**House Ruler:** Twelfth
**Color:** Violet
**The Body:** Pineal gland

Neptune is a mystical planet of dreams, spirituality, intuition, and creativity. While Neptune is wonderful for things that are sparked through imagination—like art and music—this planet also rules illusions and deception. This means that a strong Neptune in your chart can allow you to be deeply connected with the spiritual world, but you can also be deceived by others and by what you see and experience. The influence of Neptune can also give you psychic abilities that make you aware of things before they happen. Neptune is a mysterious and complex planet that holds the key to the thin veil between the subconscious and the unconscious, the seen and the unseen.

# PLUTO

## THE ONE WHO BRINGS TRANSFORMATION

·✦·

**Planet Cycle:** Spends 12 to 32 years in each sign, a 248-year cycle
**Sign Ruler:** Scorpio (modern ruler)
**House Ruler:** Eighth
**Color:** Black and dark red
**The Body:** Reproductive system, skin

Pluto rules power, transformation, death, rebirth, and the hidden parts of ourselves. In Greek mythology, Pluto is the god of the underworld and forces us to look deep inside to discover who we are and what motivates us to do the things we do in life. Pluto's influence can draw people to you like a magnet with its very strong energy (an energy that is hard to put one's finger on). It allows you to peel away the things that aren't true to your highest spiritual self and can reveal your destiny and purpose on Earth.

Part Three

# ASTROLOGICAL SIGNS & WHAT THEY MEAN

# CHAPTER NINE

# Sun, Moon & Rising Signs (SMR)

## The Big Three or the Magic Three

If you know your Sun, Moon, and Rising signs (also called the Ascendant), you're in good shape! These three signs form the foundation of your personality and identity. Your Sun sign reveals how you express yourself in the world; your Moon sign reveals how you deal with your emotions and feelings deep inside you; and your Rising sign reveals the first impression you make when others meet you. It also rules how you interact with the world. By knowing all three of your signs—and those of your family and friends—you gain a lot of information about who a person is inwardly and outwardly. You can find your Sun and Moon signs by knowing the month, day, and year you were born. You must know your *exact* birth time to find your Rising sign.

## SUN SIGNS

If someone tells you you're a Libra or Virgo, they are most likely talking about your Sun sign. The Sun sign gives a hint about a person's sense of identity in the world and their self-expression. The Sun moves into a different sign every thirty days, which is why Sun signs are tied to the month you were born. For example, if you were born March 3, you're a Pisces, but if you were born April 3, you're an Aries. The following are the twelve different Sun signs and what personality traits and qualities someone born under each sign most likely has.

# THE SUN

**Planet Cycle:** 30 days in each sign,
1-year cycle through the Zodiac
**Sign Ruler:** Leo
**Day of the Week:** Sunday
**House Ruler:** Fifth
**Colors:** Gold, yellow
**The Body:** Spine, heart

All the planets—except for the Moon—revolve around the Sun. In astrological studies, the Sun represents the parts of our personalities that drive us. It is the force that shows how we express ourselves. It takes twelve months for the Sun to enter each sign of the Zodiac. Our Sun signs last approximately one month because we are following the movement of the Sun. Since we know that the Sun sign represents our outward activities and self-expression, we can combine the astrology signs (Aries through Pisces) with the traits of the Sun to get a deeper understanding of our personalities, our ways of thinking, and our behaviors. When people are born, the placement of the Sun will always be in one of these signs, which consist of a group of stars or constellations that are in various places in the sky. For example, if the Sun is near the constellation of Gemini at the time you were born, Gemini is your Sun sign.

# SUN IN ARIES
## (MARCH 21–APRIL 20)

Symbol: The Ram
Quality: Cardinal
Element: Fire
Ruling Planet: Mars
Polarity: Masculine, Assertive
The Body: Head, face, blood
Archetype: The Warrior

### "I TAKE ACTION, AND I CAN DO ANYTHING!"

Aries is the first sign of the Zodiac! It is a cardinal Fire sign and is ruled by Mars. If you are an Aries, this means that you love new beginnings and have a lot of energy. You go after what you want without others having to push you. There is a side of you that likes to compete, whether it be in sports or being the best at school activities, and you find it fun to show the world that you are strong and capable of anything! You tend to become angry if you don't get your way and are very independent. You are more of a leader than a follower and become excited when you start new projects. And you *always* push your way to the finish line.

# SUN IN TAURUS

## (APRIL 21–MAY 20)

Symbol: The Bull
Quality: Fixed
Element: Earth
Ruling Planet: Venus
Polarity: Feminine, Receptive
The Body: Neck, throat, mouth, voice
Archetype: The Farmer

### "I WILL SUCCEED, IN TIME!"

Taurus is a fixed Earth sign that is ruled by Venus. As a Taurus, you like to take your time and work slowly but surely on things you enjoy. When you are making art or doing your homework, you like to make sure your work is done just right. It is important for you to have nice things around you, and you are kind and loyal to others. There is also a stubborn side to this sign—whose symbol is the bull. You don't like to be pushed around or controlled, but your agreeable personality allows you to get along with others easier than other signs. You are a good friend, and you expect your friends and family to be just as reliable and stable as you are.

# SUN IN GEMINI
## (MAY 21–JUNE 20)

Symbol: The Twins
Quality: Mutable
Element: Air
Ruling Planet: Mercury
Polarity: Masculine, Assertive
The Body: Arms, hands, lungs
Archetype: An Intellectual

## "EVERYTHING MAKES ME CURIOUS!"

Gemini is a mutable Air sign that is ruled by the planet Mercury. If you are a Gemini, you love to talk and get excited about thinking and learning different things. Geminis don't like to do the same things every day, however. You enjoy change and discovering different ideas and ways of doing things. You may ask a lot of questions and learn how to do things quickly. You have a good sense of humor and are fun to be around because you are interesting and lighthearted.

# SUN IN CANCER
## (JUNE 21–JULY 20)

Symbol: **The Crab**
Quality: **Cardinal**
Element: **Water**
Ruling Planet: **The Moon**
Polarity: **Feminine, Receptive**
The Body: **Stomach, chest**
Archetype: **The Poet**

### "MY EMOTIONS RUN DEEP, AND I CARE!"

The mutable Water sign of Cancer is ruled by the Moon. This makes you, as a Cancer, a very sensitive and emotional person. You like to make sure your friends and family feel safe and loved. In return, you want to feel this way as well. The symbol of Cancer is the crab. This means you are hard on the outside, but inside you are quite soft. When others hurt your feelings, you go into your inner shell and may not talk to others about how you have been hurt. This can cut you off from feeling the love of others who want to help you. You have a big heart and can sometimes know what others are feeling without them letting you know with their words. This gives you a chance to solve problems before they get out of hand.

# SUN IN LEO

## (JULY 21–AUGUST 20)

Symbol: **The Lion**
Quality: **Fixed**
Element: **Fire**
Ruling Planet: **The Sun**
Polarity: **Masculine, Assertive**
The Body: **Heart, spine**
Archetype: **Royalty**

## "ENJOY LIFE AND HAVE FUN!"

Leo is a fixed Fire sign that is ruled by the Sun. As a Leo, you are a very exciting, fun-loving person, and you love being the center of attention! Leos are symbolized by the lion. This makes you strong-willed and a good leader. You love drama and may like to dress in flashy clothes to get others to notice you. You enjoy showing people that you love them by giving them lots of affection, and you are very friendly. Many times you think you are right and don't listen when others are telling you that you are wrong. It's good to listen when you feel angry, but your sweet, giving nature helps you get through tough times.

# SUN IN VIRGO
## (AUGUST 21—SEPTEMBER 20)

Symbol: The Virgin
Quality: Mutable
Element: Earth
Ruling Planet: Mercury
Polarity: Feminine, Receptive
The Body: Intestines, spleen, solar plexus
Archetype: A Craftsperson

### "I LEARN AND AIM FOR PERFECTION!"

With the mutable Earth sign that is ruled by Mercury, a Virgo person is very down to earth and chatty. You like to do things step-by-step, meaning everything you do is done by thinking about it first and then working hard to reach your goal. You may write your homework assignments down so you can remember them—that way, you can do the absolute best job you can. You like to make sure things are perfect and get a little impatient when you must wait for others to finish what you started. You are very gentle and kind and enjoy fixing things that are broken. You like it very much when others appreciate you, and you like yourself the most when you have done a good job!

# SUN IN LIBRA
## (SEPTEMBER 21–OCTOBER 20)

Symbol: The Scales
Quality: Cardinal
Element: Air
Ruling Planet: Venus
Polarity: Masculine, Assertive
The Body: Kidneys, bladder, skin
Archetype: The Judge

### "I NEED BALANCE TO BE HAPPY!"

Libra is a cardinal Air sign ruled by Venus. As such, you love to be surrounded by beautiful things. Libra is the sign of relationships, so you like to spend time with your friends and family, and you can get along with just about anyone! You are very smart and friendly and make people feel better when they are sad. You do not like to get into arguments and prefer to be in a loving environment. You may find that you most enjoy wearing nice clothes, having your hair done, and showing your sparkling smile to all who cross your path. All Air signs like to use their brains and show how smart they are when doing schoolwork. Libras can wait until the last minute to do things. You can also have a hard time making decisions, but when it comes to your friends, you are very fair and graceful.

# SUN IN SCORPIO

## (OCTOBER 21–NOVEMBER 20)

Symbol: **The Scorpion**
Quality: **Fixed**
Element: **Water**
Ruling Planet: **Pluto**
Polarity: **Feminine, Receptive**
The Body: **Reproductive system**
Archetype: **The Magician**

### "I AM INTENSE AND EXPLORE DEEP EMOTIONS!"

Scorpio is a fixed Water sign ruled by Pluto. When you are born under this sign, you tend to be passionate, and your feelings are deep and intense. You can be very secretive and don't always like to tell the truth about what you are thinking or feeling. When angry, it is possible that you will say very hurtful things to others without considering how your words might affect them. You can act very controlling and possessive, not wanting to share your friends' and family's love and affection with others. When you are having a deep feeling, you should breathe and count to ten or go to a quiet place to cool down so you don't end up making those around you sad or angry. Scorpios are also deeply loving people and can have strong and lasting friendships when they feel comfortable with their friends.

# SUN IN SAGITTARIUS
## (NOVEMBER 21–DECEMBER 20)

Symbol: **The Centaur**
Quality: **Mutable**
Element: **Fire**
Ruling Planet: **Jupiter**
Polarity: **Masculine, Assertive**
The Body: **Thighs, liver, gallbladder**
Archetype: **The High Priest**

**"LIFE IS AN ADVENTURE AND A PATHWAY TO TRUTH!"**

Sagittarius is a mutable Fire sign that is ruled by Jupiter. If you are a Sagittarius, you are a very kind and outgoing person who loves freedom and independence. You like to do things your own way and aren't the type of person who likes to sit in the house all day. You crave adventure and fun! You can be outspoken and say exactly what is on your mind, not holding anything back. This doesn't get in the way of you being fun and enjoyable to be around, though. Sagittarians can be generous, meaning you like to share with others to make them happy. You aren't always looking for people to give you things in return.

# SUN IN CAPRICORN
## (DECEMBER 21–JANUARY 20)

Symbol: **The Mountain Goat**
Quality: **Cardinal**
Element: **Earth**
Ruling Planet: **Saturn**
Polarity: **Feminine, Receptive**
The Body: **Knees, bones, teeth, nails**
Archetype: **The Hermit**

### "I AM RESPONSIBLE AND RELIABLE!"

Capricorn is a cardinal Earth sign ruled by Saturn. You, as a Capricorn, can be very serious about getting things done. You like to follow the rules, and the things you learn help you determine right from wrong. You tend to enjoy spending time with grown-ups more than kids your own age because they can teach you things and show you how to be strong in the world. Playing outside just for the fun of it doesn't make that much sense to you. Instead, you like to know that what you are doing has a purpose and will lead you to having success in your schoolwork. You also enjoy being responsible by helping your parents and friends. You will need to work a little harder to have a little bit more fun in life and are sure to find that it won't interfere with you learning things.

# SUN IN AQUARIUS

## (JANUARY 21–FEBRUARY 20)

Symbol: **The Water Bearer**
Quality: **Fixed**
Element: **Air**
Ruling Planet: **Uranus**
Polarity: **Masculine, Assertive**
The Body: **Ankles, calves, pancreas**
Archetype: **The Wise Fool**

### "I HAVE A HUNGER FOR KNOWLEDGE AND NEW THINGS!"

As the fixed Air sign ruled by Uranus, Aquarians thrive on friendship and in groups, but at the same time, they are very independent. You stand strong in your beliefs, and you don't like it when people try to fence you in with rules or a particular way of doing things. You like to show your uniqueness and individuality and can't stand to be like everyone else. You are smart and friendly and like sharing what you think more than sharing your inner feelings. You can be a little detached from the world around you as you live in your head, making up new games, drawing pictures, and telling stories that you imagine with your creative mind. Aquarians are fun-loving, kind people. People from different backgrounds tend to be drawn to your unique worldview!

# SUN IN PISCES

## (FEBRUARY 21—MARCH 20)

Symbol: Two Fishes
Quality: Mutable
Element: Water
Ruling Planet: Neptune
Polarity: Feminine, Receptive
The Body: Feet, ankles
Archetype: The Profit

### "MY SPIRITUALITY IS THE MOST IMPORTANT THING TO ME!"

Pisces is a mutable Water sign ruled by Neptune. As a Pisces, you are a dreamer who is very sensitive. You live in your feelings and have an ability to pick up on the feelings and moods of the people in whatever room you're in. You are very creative and are drawn to the arts like music, dance, writing, and theater. You care very much for people who are hurting, and you like to make others feel better. You believe in being a good person, and it is very important to you to help your family and friends with loving advice, sweet hugs, and gifts. Sometimes you like to run away to a private place when your feelings are hurt. But if you truly want others to support you, you must try to tell them how you're feeling, so they can be as kind to you as you are to them.

## MOON SIGNS

A person's Moon sign can tell you about that individual's emotions and feel-ings. Your Moon sign is calculated by the position of the Moon at your time of birth. You can find your own Moon sign by knowing the month, day, and year you were born. It takes the Moon two-and-a-half days to travel to each sign. Because of that, your best friend's birthday could be five days before your birthday, but you'll have different Moon signs! Cool, huh? If you know someone with the Moon in Pisces, you can predict that this person may feel very deeply and can have a soft and mystical way of seeing the world.

If someone's Moon is in Virgo, they may be more interested in solving their emotional problems through planning and action rather than by crying or getting visibly upset. Knowing your Moon sign can help you work through some painful things that go on in your heart and mind, and it can also help you find the beautiful parts of yourself so you can love *you* more and more every day!

You can find out your Moon sign by knowing the month, day, and year you were born. You can figure out your Moon sign by visiting this free website: *https://horoscopes.astro-seek.com/which-moon-phase-was-i-born-under-calcu lator.* Be sure to ask your parents or an older family member for help when doing the calculations!

Note: If you don't know your birth time, that's okay. Just add 12:00 a.m. or 12:00 p.m. for the time. Your calculation will still be correct!

## THE MOON

Planet Cycle: 2½ days in each sign,
28-day cycle through the Zodiac
Sign Ruler: Cancer
Day of the Week: Monday
House Ruler: Fourth
Color: Silver
The Body: Stomach, chest

The Moon represents our emotions and inner thoughts. It teaches us about the deeper parts of our mind and how we connect to the world and others through our feelings and the more private parts of ourselves that we aren't always aware of. Knowing which Zodiac constellation the Moon was in when you were born will help you better understand the ways you express your emotions.

## MOON IN ARIES

When your Moon is in Aries, it means you are strong, independent, and stand up for your beliefs! With this Mars-ruled sign, you may have a bit of a temper when you don't get what you want. Your strength helps you express your feelings honestly and powerfully.

## MOON IN TAURUS

If your Moon is in the Venus-ruled sign of Taurus, you are patient, slow to anger, and have a very dependable way of showing your feelings. Your mother and family are probably stable, which means you don't have a lot of crazy changes in your home that are tough to handle. You love people in a calm and grounded way, and others see you as a giving, respectful, and easygoing person.

## MOON IN GEMINI

The Mercury-ruled Gemini Moon sign makes you a very smart and witty person! Your emotions can change quickly, and you like to think about things more than feel them. Your mother and home may be surrounded by a lot of talking, fun conversations, and intelligent ways of solving problems. You may have a hard time getting in touch with your emotions as you like to think about all the ideas you have instead of crying or getting upset when you have something you need to figure out.

## MOON IN CANCER

Cancer is ruled by the Moon! Having Cancer as your Moon sign makes you the most emotional and mothering sign of all the Zodiac. Your mother is probably very kind, loving, protective, and makes sure that she puts her family before her own needs in order to be happy. The Moon in Cancer makes you comfortable with your feelings and the feelings of others. You may give your family members a hug when they are feeling sad, and you do your very best to make others feel safe and loved.

## MOON IN LEO

With the Sun-ruled sign of Leo in your Moon placement, you are a person who loves attention! Your mom and family may shower you with love, and your home might be filled with parties, family dinners, and a lot of love toward you. You enjoy being friendly and getting showered with compliments, sweet words about your artwork, and many loving hugs. You like for all eyes to be on you while you show your friends and family your new dance moves or a song you learned in school.

## MOON IN VIRGO

The Moon in Mercury-ruled Virgo makes it hard for you to share your feelings. Your mother and family are probably very serious, and there may not be a lot of emotion shared around the house. You like to show your love and feelings through actions and sharing instead of telling someone you love them straight-out. You may help your family with the housework or clean your room and get good grades to show how much you love and appreciate them for taking care of you.

## MOON IN LIBRA

The Venus-ruled Libra as your Moon sign makes you a very gentle and kind person. Your mom and home may be filled with sweetness and heartfelt connections. Your mother may stay away from large arguments and heated discussions. Seeing the best in others is the way you're taught to get along with the world. If your home is loud and brash, you may choose to smooth things over by giving a smile and exiting the situation to go and play computer games or read a book. You like to think more than have deep feelings, but there's a lot of love in your heart!

## MOON IN SCORPIO

If your Moon is in the Pluto-ruled sign of Scorpio, you may feel your emotions very deeply but have a hard time showing them. Your mother and home may have a very quiet and secretive energy to them. You don't like to talk about what's going on inside your heart and mind. Your feelings may be so strong that you think others must know how you're feeling so there's no need to share them. It's good to be honest and to express yourself to your family, though, so don't feel shy when you are going through a hard time, and always ask for help.

## MOON IN SAGITTARIUS

Having the Jupiter-ruled sign of Sagittarius as your Moon placement means you are a very cheerful and intelligent person. Your mother and home may offer you a lot of freedom, letting you run free in the park and decide what you want for dinner and how to cook it! You love finding out the truth and are very honest about your feelings. Sometimes, you can be a bit brash when sharing your emotions, and you might hurt other people's feelings. This doesn't mean you shouldn't be honest. Just keep in mind that the way you see and feel things is important, but not everyone can handle talking about deep emotions the way you can.

## MOON IN CAPRICORN

The Saturn-ruled sign of Capricorn in your Moon sign makes you a serious person who doesn't like to share your emotions. Your mother and home may have taught you to do well in school, save any money you may receive, and work hard. If your home is very messy or disorganized, you may decide to be more responsible and keep your feelings buried deep inside. You may show your feelings through achievements like winning awards in karate, dance troop, or other activities you love. Try not to be focused on the things you achieve but rather share your emotions if you are having painful or loving feelings.

## MOON IN AQUARIUS

With the Moon in Uranus-ruled Aquarius you love to be different! Your mom and home may be filled with interesting conversations that help you grow and expand your imagination. You like to come up with fun ideas that help you change the world. (Maybe you'd like to be class president so you can advocate for healthier school lunches, for example.) You are not the most emotional person, as you prefer to express yourself through your ideas and the ways you can bring positive change to your home and neighborhood. Be the amazing inventor you were meant to be!

## MOON IN PISCES

The Neptune-ruled sign of Pisces as your Moon sign causes you to be very in touch with your emotions. Your mother and home may be calm and careful about hurting others' feelings. If your home is full of arguments, you may have learned to be kind and care for others instead. Pisces are known to be intuitive and psychic, meaning you can feel what others are feeling, which makes you know how to help others when they are having a hard time. You have a lot of compassion and want everyone in your life to feel safe and loved.

## RISING SIGNS

Your Rising sign, or Ascendant, is one of the most important signs, along with the Sun and the Moon signs, that reveals crucial things about your personality. It reveals your outward approach to life and some aspects of your personality that people immediately notice about you. If you are a Sagittarius Rising, others may notice that you are very outgoing and independent, even if your Sun and Moon signs are represented by Zodiac signs that are a bit more quiet and shy. Others may think you are fun loving when they first meet you because of your Sagittarius Rising sign. As they get to know you and learn more about your personality and emotions, they will see aspects of your Sun and Moon signs—but the Rising sign shines through first!

To find out your Rising sign (the sign that was positioned on the eastern horizon the moment you are born) and which of your planets are in each of the houses (sometimes there can be no planets in a house or sometimes there are two), you will need to know the month, day, and year of your birth as well as the exact time you were born. You need to know your birth time because the Rising sign moves through the Zodiac every two hours. A difference of just a few minutes can change your entire chart because of the faster moving planets and the quickness with which the Rising sign moves. Two people can be born thirty minutes apart and have different Rising signs! It all depends on the place the planets were sitting the exact moment you were born!

It will be hard to know exactly which signs and planets sit in each of your houses without knowing your birth time. But don't worry if you can't find your birth time. Just remember it is an especially important part of the astrological puzzle that you may want to find out in the future.

## ARIES RISING

You are a born leader! Your Aries Rising sign gives you the inner strength to do whatever you set your mind to. You are most interested in what you think and want, and you care less about others' motivations. You can be very competitive and want to win at everything you do. Aries Risings tend to be impatient and a bit self-centered. You don't like waiting around for things to happen, and you can have a bit of a temper! Even though you may be quick to anger, you cool off quickly and don't stay angry for very long. You are courageous, passionate, and strong-willed. You are not great at compromising with others, so make an extra effort to listen to people's ideas before you strike out on your own.

## TAURUS RISING

Taurus Risings like to stick to what they know. It is hard for you to feel comfortable in new environments, and you like to move slowly and thoughtfully before making decisions. You are kind and charming, and you draw people near to you by your loving, earthy energy. You like to make others comfortable with your easygoing personality, and you are interested in living in safe and stable environments. You enjoy the comfort of beautiful things and love good food, nice clothing, and all the delights the world has to offer.

## GEMINI RISING

Gemini Risings love to make friends and are interested in talking to many different people! You are very smart and witty, which makes it easy for you to get along in all types of situations and environments. You are mostly interested in learning and like all forms of communication. You tend to get quite bored when you are not stimulated, which makes you set out to find something new and exciting to keep you interested. You draw people to you with your fun, friendly, and adaptable personality.

## CANCER RISING

When entering a new environment, others may see you as shy and withdrawn. Cancer Rising people need to feel safe and secure before they try something new. This means you may hold back or stay home from a party or gathering if you don't know exactly who will be there or what the energy of the room will be like. You have a mothering approach to life and are very sensitive and emotional. You like to make others feel nurtured but expect others to make you feel comfortable in return. You do not like conflict and try not to get into disagreements. You draw people to you with your soft heart and genuine nature.

## LEO RISING

Leo Risings love the limelight! You thrive on meeting people. When you are at your best, people feel happy and comfortable as they bask in your kind and delightful energy. You can have a dramatic personality and love to be the center of attention. You care about others' feelings, and it is important that other people return that same kindness to you. You are a very trustworthy person and are loyal to your friends and family. When others are not kind to you, you stand up for yourself and let them know that you require respect and lasting friendships.

## VIRGO RISING

When faced with a new environment, Virgo Risings feel most comfortable in educational situations. You like to take in everything that is going on around you, but you can be a little shy in social surroundings. It is important for you to have things in order, and you tend to draw people in with your practical personality. You like for things to be perfect, and you work very hard to create a neat and tidy environment for yourself and others. You are open to people sharing their ideas with you, as long as they are grounded and make sense in your mind. Your flair for order makes you a good person to work with!

## LIBRA RISING

Libra Risings are very charming and love to look their best. You are very social, and you draw people in with your sweet and outgoing personality. You get along with many different personalities and enjoy beautiful surroundings filled with friendly people. When approaching new situations, you use your intelligence more than your emotions. It is important for people to be just as smart and kind as you are so that you feel equal and comfortable in your environment. You love to share and have an eye for pleasing clothing, music, and people.

## SCORPIO RISING

When Scorpio is your Rising sign you tend to feel out new environments with your intuition. You can see below the surface of things, pick up on small details others might miss, and guess the motivations of those around you. You are more comfortable with your inward emotions and feel a bit out of place where there are loud and super outgoing personalities. You quietly observe your environment. People are drawn to you for your deep thoughts and ability to understand the subtle flow of life. Although you can be quiet, you also have a powerful energy that helps you decide which situations are best for you.

## SAGITTARIUS RISING

Sagittarius Rising people are independent and outgoing. You have a bright outlook on life and the future, and people are drawn to you because you have a sunny and friendly personality. You don't like to be held down by commitments and prefer to be free to do whatever you like whenever you like. You are curious and adventurous and see new situations and environments as excellent opportunities to experience something new and exciting.

## CAPRICORN RISING

If you are a Capricorn Rising, you are hardworking, responsible, and a bit shy. You approach new situations cautiously and might come off as a bit withdrawn to people when you first meet them. You take a little more time than other signs to warm up to strangers and have a hard time feeling comfortable in new environments. Your serious personality may cause you to feel safest around older people who can guide and protect you. Others will be drawn to your serious personality and find you to be strong and organized.

## AQUARIUS RISING

Aquarius Risings are very intelligent and have a kind and inviting personality. You love to share your ideas with many different people. Others are drawn to you because you are inventive and think outside the box. You love to create new things that challenge the old ways of doing things. You feel most comfortable in environments that afford you a lot of freedom to think, change, and learn. Nonetheless, when you find something that you truly believe in, it will be very hard to get you to change your mind and take a different approach. Your personality is attractive and stimulating.

## PISCES RISING

Pisces Risings are one of the most sensitive signs of the Zodiac. It takes time for you to feel comfortable in new environments, but your compassionate and loving personality draws people to you. It is important for you to find the best qualities in people, and you tend to see the beauty in others instead of their darker sides. You like to help others and make them feel safe and calm, as you share a very intuitive and peaceful environment when you are comfortable. You have a vivid imagination, and you share your vision with softness and without judgment.

# CHAPTER TEN

# Calculating Your Chart

As you've learned in the previous chapters, when you know your signs, planets, and houses, you can begin to interpret your own birth chart. You will be able to go through this book as you read your chart and make the connections to what the signs and planets in your houses mean. There are also some tools that can help you learn how to read your chart by giving you interpretations of how the placements of the signs and planets relate to one another.

There are also useful apps like *Time Passages*, *Time Nomad*, and *Co-Star* that will create your astrology chart for you! Not only will they create the chart, but these apps will tell you about specific important aspects of your chart like your Sun, Moon, and Rising signs, your planets, and what is going on in your chart during the current day. You can check your horoscope and chart before you go to school so you can be prepared. For example, you can be prepared by knowing if Mars is making everyone grumpy or if Neptune is making your friends and teachers feel dreamy and hazy.

You will be able to learn and study your chart from your or your parent's phone, but it is also especially important to read books. There are great books like *The Junior Astrologer's Handbook* by Nikki Van De Car and *Starring You: A Guided Journey Through Astrology* by Aliza Kelly that can help you continue your journey of discovery. Although you might not be a teenager yet, there's a great article in *Teen Vogue* called "How to Read Your Birth Chart" that is a great resource to read online!

If you would like to have an astrologer read your astrology chart for you, your parents can help you schedule a reading from *BlackGirlHoroscope.com*. Astrology readings can be quite expensive, so don't be hurt if your parents are not able to afford it. There are many ways to learn astrology. Make sure you read, study, and memorize this book before you ask your parents to spend lots of money on additional readings and tools.

## PUTTING IT ALL TOGETHER

Wow, you have learned so much about astrology! Remember that this is a beginner's guide, so you'll want to make sure you study this book before you move on to learning more about reading birth charts, which is a skill that's going to help you make deeper predictions by learning things like transits, conjunctions, sextiles, squares, and oppositions. It's okay if you don't know what these words mean yet; you're still learning!

Everything in this book is included to give you the best foundational knowledge of astrology so you can keep studying if you want. It also celebrates your Black Girl Magic ability—you can use this book to start changing the world! When you study astrology, you gain wisdom that helps you get along with others and become a fair and caring leader. You will understand how to deal with people's different personality traits and communication styles. Leadership starts with being able to understand people.

You know which signs are based in which elements and quadruplicities, and you have learned how planets rule the signs, how long these planets stay in each sign, and what house each sign rules.

With all this information saved in your memory, you'll be well on your way to becoming a well-rounded student of astrology. You may begin to see patterns in your life based on your astrological knowledge. Have fun trying to guess people's signs based on their personalities and be sure to tell your friends how each planet affects their lives.

Don't try to rush any of this, however! It will all come together in due time. You can write down notes in your astrology journal (all you need is a notebook!) to remember as you read and reread the book; you can ask others to quiz you to help you study; and you can even make flash cards for easy reference. Every day you study you'll be a step closer to being an astrology whiz kid!

Don't forget to thank everyone who helps you along the way. And don't forget to thank and love yourself for being an intelligent and amazing Black girl! You've got this!

# Select Glossary

**Astrology:** the study of how the stars, planets, and other celestial bodies influence people and how they act based on their positions in space

**Astronomy:** the study of objects such as planets, stars, moons, and more in outer space

**Almanac:** a book that publishes information about the movement of the Sun and Moon and is often published once a year

**Birth Chart:** a document that describes astrological influences on a person based on that person's time and place of birth

**Celestial:** describing or related to objects in the sky or space (such as the Sun, Moon, and stars)

**Chart Ruler:** the planet that rules over a person's Rising sign and predicts what will have the most influence in their life

**Constellations:** collections of stars in the sky that have been given particular names based on how they look (and are especially noted around the time of a person's birth)

**Equinox:** one of two times a year (spring/vernal and fall/autumnal) when the Sun is directly over the Earth's equator, and day and night everywhere on the Earth are exactly the same length

**Galaxy:** a large gathering of stars and other objects that are found throughout the universe (our galaxy is called the Milky Way)

**Horoscope:** a method in which astrologers can see the position of the planets and signs of the Zodiac at a particular time of year and then predict a person's personality traits and future events in their life determined through astrology, depending on the person's exact date, time, and location of birth

**Natal Chart:** also called a birth chart and used in astrology to reveal aspects of a person's life and personality based on the exact location of planets and other celestial bodies at the time of someone's birth

**Orbit:** a path that's traveled by one celestial body around another

**Polarity:** being drawn to a certain object or in a certain direction

**Prediction:** an art of looking ahead into the future and foretelling what may happen to someone or something

**Sign:** in astrology, this refers to one of twelve aspects of the Zodiac

**Zodiac:** a band of the celestial sky that is divided into twelve constellations or signs used for astrological predictions and study

# Charts

## THE ZODIAC

ARIES

TAURUS

GEMINI

CANCER

LEO

VIRGO

LIBRA

SCORPIO

SAGITTARIUS

CAPRICORN

AQUARIUS

PISCES

# THE HOUSES

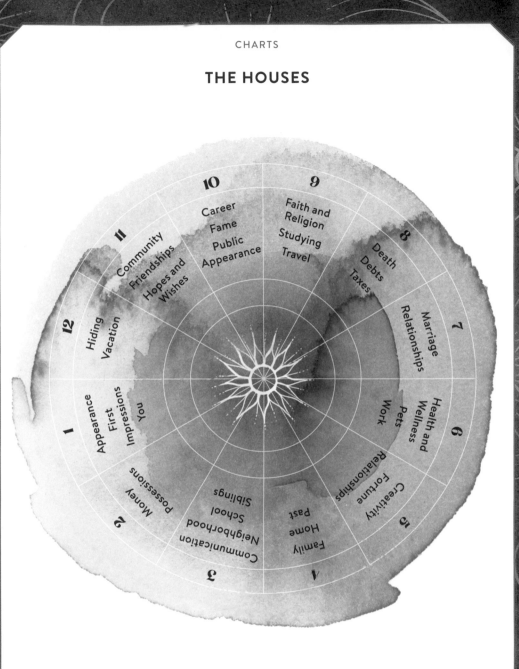

**10** Career / Fame / Public Appearance

**9** Faith and Religion / Studying / Travel

**11** Community / Friendships / Hopes and Wishes

**8** Death / Debts / Taxes

**12** Hiding / Vacation

**7** Marriage / Relationships

**1** Appearance / First Impressions / You

**6** Health and Wellness / Pets / Work

**2** Money / Possessions

**5** Creativity / Fortune / Relationships

**3** Communication / Neighborhood / School / Siblings

**4** Family / Home / Past

# THE PLANETS

SUN

MERCURY

VENUS

EARTH

MOON

MARS

JUPITER

SATURN

URANUS

NEPTUNE

CERES

PLUTO

# Bibliography

Banzhaf, Hajo, and Anna Haebler. *Key Words for Astrology.* York Beach, ME: Weiser Books, 1996.

Farebrother, Sue Merlyn. *Astrology Decoded: A Step-by-Step Guide to Learning Astrology.* London, UK: Rider, 2013.

Faulkner, Carolyn. *The Signs.* New York: Ballantine Books, 2017.

Levine, Joyce. *Breakthrough Astrology.* San Francisco, CA: Weiser Books, 2006.

Parker, Julia, and Derek Parker. *Parkers' Encyclopedia of Astrology.* London, UK: Watkins Publishing, 2009.

Pond, David. *Astrology for Beginners.* Woodbury, MN: Llewellyn Publications, 2020.

Woodfolk, Joanna Martine. *The Only Astrology Book You'll Ever Need.* Lanham, MD: Madison Books, 2021.

# Acknowledgments

I'd like to thank Samuel Reynolds for returning my email so quickly and being an absolute leader for the Black astrology community. I'd also like to thank the International Society of Black Astrologers Facebook group for being a wonderful way to connect with other Black astrologers from all over the world.

The staff of the Benjamin Banneker Historical Park and Museum was very helpful in my research of Banneker's astrological inclusions in his almanac.

Acyuta-Bhava Das has been my online astrological guide and teacher from afar. I was made aware of his work and teachings through an angel of a friend who took his first-year ancient astrology course, and it has made a big difference in my life.

It is important that I acknowledge Linda Goodman, who I have been reading since I was a girl, and Liz Greene, who I have also enjoyed reading since I can remember. They had a hand in bringing astrology to a mainstream audience, and if that is too generous, they changed the game for me when it came to love astrology, compatibility, and synastry with their books *Love Signs* and *Relationship Signs* (Goodman) and *Astrology for Lovers* (Greene). These books may seem a little campy now that I have learned more about synastry, but they brought hours of joy as I explored the books in depth over the last nearly twenty years.

I'm very appreciative of all the Black women mystics, entrepreneurs, and astrologists who have leveraged social media to launch their businesses, whether they be astrological chart readings and courses or online marketplaces for crystals and supplemental tools to accompany astrological study, or who just write amazing horoscopes and analysis on their feeds. I see you and I hope that you all get the opportunity I have now to write freely about astrology.

I'm thankful for my editor Julie Matysik and Running Press Kids for believing in me and collaborating to make *Astrology for Black Girls* possible. If you would have told me twenty years ago I'd be writing the book that I so desperately needed when I was a girl, I might not have believed it. Life works in mysterious ways. I've always been connected to astrology, and it has brought me far in life. I only hope this book will bring other girls as much joy as my studies have brought me.

I'd like to thank my mother for never judging me or stopping me from pursuing the study of astrology when I was a young girl around twelve years old. I would sit in the aisles of bookstores and read astrology books for hours while she browsed. What would have become of me if she did not support me? Would I be as empathetic, understanding, and emotionally intelligent? Would I understand compatibility and pursue healthy relationships without the knowledge I have of how the planets and stars connect us and bring us together as long- and short-term soul mates? Would I be as grounded if I didn't know of my Capricorn Rising sign, or as patient with the passion that stirs in me because of my Aries moon? I don't know who I would have become without my supportive and nonjudgmental mother. She is a Scorpio and I love her for it.

# About the Author and Illustrator

**Jordannah Elizabeth** has studied astrology since she was twelve years old. She is inspired by the teachings of Acyuta-Bhava Das, Sam Reynolds, and astrologers of color who strive to create a space for diversity and inclusion in the study of Western modern astrology and ancient astrology.

**Chellie Carroll** has loved to draw ever since being able to hold chunky crayons and defacing her bedroom walls with them. After studying Applied Arts at the University of Derby and a brief spell working as a designer within the retail industry, Chellie turned to illustration and hasn't looked back. She now lives in Peak District with her partner and two children, working from her home studio where she is surrounded by the beautiful, inspirational countryside and a plentiful supply of tea and biscuits.

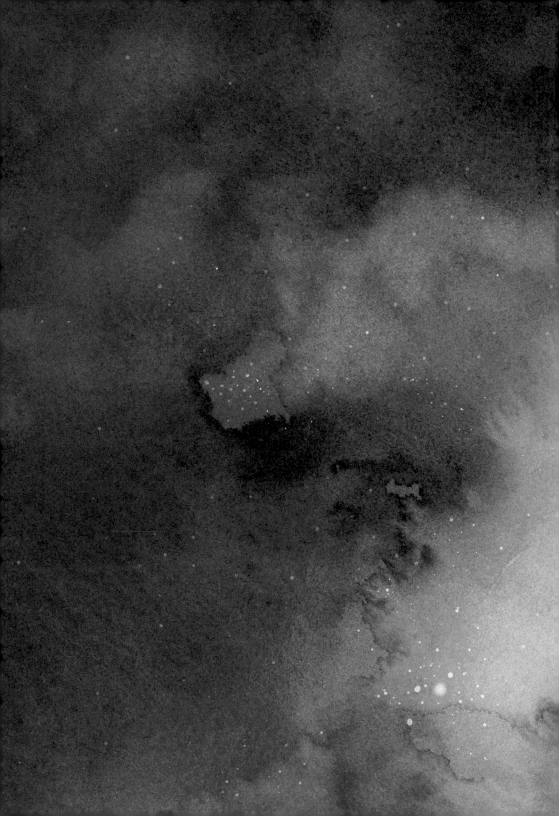